EGO DIVINUS

Parmenides' Answer, 2009, acrylic on canvas. Courtesy of the author.

EGO DIVINUS

POEMS IN ORDER
AS THEY WERE WRITTEN

Fred Wellner

FIELD STONE PRESS

Copyright © 2010 by Frederick A. Wellner
All Rights Reserved

Field Stone Press
2970 Lafayette Road
Lafayette, NY 13084
onemind@twcny.rr.com

First Edition 2010
10 11 12 13 14 15   6 5 4 3 2 1

EAN-13 9780982491638

This is a work of poetry from the gut.
Any presumed reference to people alive or dead,
otherwordly, etc., is purely coincidental.

No part of this book may be reproduced, by any means now known
or to be invented, without the written permission of the author, except by
a reviewer who wishes to quote short passages for use in a review publication.

Ego Divinus
was designed and composed in 10/14' Sabon
by Field Stone Press.

To my Dad

FRED WELLNER is an artist, writer, and a student of Religion and Philosophy at Syracuse University. He is the author of *Dead Again*, and *SYN*, also by Field Stone Press.

Whosoever conquers others has force.
Whosoever conquers himself is strong.

--Lao Tzu

EGO DIVINUS

Ego Divinus

Baleful eye
Inward monster of the deep
You know nothing
And everything
All that water and unable to drink

My soul laid bare
And yet you fail
Your existence mine
My plight is thine
You fear the Leviathan

Triumph pointless
The Ocean teems
Yet the sea is her own master
We her wayward bastards
The hunger of Cronos against us

How can you judge,
Who knows the heart?
It is the sea that
casts us adrift
For good or ill she confides not.

I turn mine eye back upon thee basilisk
Fore and aft my rudder cares not
I am made from dust, but you—
You are of what made the dust, t'is true
And your youth betrays itself, unguided but watched.

Here, Now, This

This thin wall of flesh between light and darkness
I'd have the light could I grasp it yet
your blindness is mine, it is ours
and with these questions we while away the hours
Men long dead give voice to their calling
My day and yours is night to them
is it so strange that they should rule?
And here we walk and talk like fools
There is a border here, thin and strong
a spider's strand, no more
yet it connects and denies
we can only draw from truth and lies
So why say God or god? Universe or One?
Existence is as Existence does.
Seek yes, but bear not
fools' cloaks o'er truth's jot

Harsh Master Smith

Of the many circles traveled here
by me, by you, this one grinds
Am I steel? Then life is stone.
My edge can only take so much hone.
Once I was bright, white or near so
then straw, yellow, orange, red
quenched in waters until my light
was well hidden from thy sight
Does the maker wish again
to see what it has covered
to touch that star within
by applying harsh abrasive spin?
No, tis the fire you must stoke
to slowly break the mule
The steel that you torture now
but puts the sweat upon thy brow
Why seek an edge past its best?
What good the brittle core?
Make, unmake, as you will
My silence testament to what you kill.

Our just desserts

Satisfaction guaranteed
is what they sell
A bold excursion
into hell
they who dare
to vent their hurt
the devil's kin
as bad as dirt
pictures proof
an endless train
of other's woes
far worse than rain
I'll take my cup
and pour it out
on the shoes of sunshine
if I've no clout
for pain must answer
the bill it runs up
When sunshine gives freely
I'll fill my cup.

The Veil's Secret

Is my existence naught but for them?
Their union, my spark, one and the same?
Did not the vastness behind the veil
Include my presence, my will, my name?
I tell you I lived, and live and will live,
eternal as heaven, mired as hell.
And if me, then you, the truth we must give
As we drink deep from this bottomless well.
You and I know the forgotten, forsaken,
Turn away if you will, the pain is great.
But heed well the beauty, the glory of truth.
Sooner or later we walk through its gate.

The Fool Knows

We look for God
Can God find himself?
If we are part of the body
The hand seeks
What the foot stumbles over
And in the darkness
tongue lashing
ears deaf
Eyes seeing narrowly
God laughs.

Wary

My cynacism is frothy,
and rich,
and poisonous,
A concoction steeped
in the cauldron of frustrated
inabilitiy to change what outweighs me.
Every plowshare
becomes
a sword
raised by
every hand
within the horde.
God sends his men and women to their dooms
each message swept by practiced brooms.
Does change come?
Good prevail?
Outlive the line
where flesh meets nail?
…
I don't know.
How can I?
The noise of mankind
deafens.

To Live

Hate is an axe, a bloody maul
Love is the tender touch, and standing tall
The line between, a human one
All the pressure of the sun
What God exists? The answer exists.
No devil but our own, the one who resists
Compassion.
There is matter, and there is nothing.
Look long enough and you'll find something.
Stagnant ponds our minds risk becoming
Sleep decays the sound of distant drumming
Climb the mountain, discover the sky
Go! Fetch the clouds or die
Trying.

All of Us

Come
Make this footprint with me
Light and deep, our ugly beauty
Forest
Gone forever, reservations of green
Everything in its place, legacy of us

Only the clouds will not be tamed
Their rain will wash away
Some of our stain
And where water fails, the wind will come
Dry and hot, it will
Erase where we were in vain.

Ira

In the blood boiling
quiet, rolling, nowhere is egress
no ear wants a taste
of this vinegar.
No eye discerns, only judges
better the dark
Does the light seem wise?
I tell you,
Only in the sun
Can the hand see to throw a true stone
Night harbors many hidden souls
And not without good reason
But this path
Causes feet to stumble
I am not wise
T'is better not to despise
What is better then?
The bright fire of a false sun
Or the dead cold where there is none?
Better my tongue twitch not.

My Road and Your Road

Today I walked the hidden rail
Ignorant…and in emptiness
that harbored something lost
not all emptiness is void or without return

The one who woke and found himself
maybe didn't have the final truth
yet he long ago turned over a stone
and there was the inference of much to learn

At the core was a truth without an owner
What claim could one make
on the convergence of paths?
How can the hand clasp the world that turns?

One can listen at many doors
And come away with what one needs
What is whispered or sung out loud
Is no more than wood for what eternally burns

Gone by the time the ear has heard
By the time the mind has absorbed
The ghost of an imprint upon the hearer
And no more needed but that it, too, has changed.

Monkey Poo

Be myself? You're kidding right?
That life raft of tolerance does not hold air
Let out my primordial shout
And I'm stoned into a dis-re-pair
A voice said "You ne'er know what will come out of his mouth."
My retort: You'll never ask meaning, so why be demeaning?
When your wish for wavelessness
Pains me with your bravelessness.
And then what changes
In the world?
You've created the excuse
To throw your stone.
Look up.
Everyone else has stones too.

Cherry Pit

The pie arrives
Sweet color oozing from cracks
Enticing my eager fork.
Break the crust.
It is more than I expected
Asked for in a last, hopeful bid.
Eagerly I fall upon it
For it is mine, my faith restored.
Blissful taste, I swallow,
Eat before it grows cool.
And there I swallow the trap
Stone in throat I die a fool.

The Box

These walls were built by others
But blame me if you must
They surround me on all sides
I am trapped and without trust
My decay is daily in this hollow place
Cage the beast, preserve you
Yet you want it both ways
That I cannot do
Understand that these walls
Surround on all sides
Each brick a hypocracy
Of conflicting tides
I am chained to the bottom
And told to swim towards the sun
I cannot drown or live
The paths you offer are none.

Fortold Resistance Fortold

Today I realized a truth
A whisper I've heard all my life
To hope is expected
Against futility's sudden knife
Who can say for whom it will strike?
We can surmise, and submit
But to lay down surely brings us
All the sooner to the quit.
It is all there is
This hope, this weakly thrown die
What number comes up is already there
And we've known forever yet still we try
To pull the web without breaking it
To move the stone so heavy
Hoping, yes, there it is again
That word knows nothing of levy
That, my friend, gets paid either way
It matters not your pocket's hole
Enter this world naked, leave it the same way
We've all one thing for collateral
But I went tangential, distracted yes
From this truth I said I've known
I can try to shake the tree
But apples fall or not, all on their own.

It Figures

What have I to offer?
Talent, a gift, says use me.
And so I do, and now have learned
The cosmos denies the fruits of its gift
Cuts the tree, forgets to water it
Or cares not
And where here exists a desert dry, full of bones and thorns
Some ways off, here and there, fountains gush and gurgle
Streams run
Thirst is not known
The way there is impassable to me
The crevasse too deep, the wall too high
I have no wings for
They've been clipped before
I could have used them to fly.

Late

When I was ripe
There was no hand
No mouth to bite
No eye to alight
In withered form
I feel the touch
The judging eyes discern
Faded color
Sweetness past and lost
And there I am left to hang
To brown and fall
My seeds to spill
This is my worth.

Compass

Stand and face the eastern sun
Where did your convictions run?
When and who and what to blame?
It's weakness now that you should shun.

Gather wit and hold it tight
Abandon it and they were right.
Curse the dark or feel your way,
Turn and face the eastern light

Circle

Breath, in and out
Blood pumps to the rhythm
of the universe, and
few see more than a kaleidoscopic prism.
But that's alright
Think not that it is but part of the beat
and melody, listen, or play you shall
what difference from the love-making of cold and heat?
What enters, exits, and returns.
What ant not a Brahma someday
and every Brahma humbled
by the cycle of existence every day?

Gravity

I fly not off into
darkness clad naked
rooted for now, able
to learn what is sacred
If this is prison
what is the disgrace?
This one wall
my feet must embrace.
For if I was ready
I'd be out there
with the stars
that hold my stare.
What I have
is to fill my cup
and to empty it also
Is that so tough?
To defeat myself
and gain something better
trade fool for the sage
that is the matter.

Threshold

At the cusp, cut or balance
Know that it is the challenge
Pass the veil, cut the cord
Anyone at all can jam your word
Before the tree bears its fruit
Before your plans lay their root
Math maps every minute
It's you against the finish
Lay your bridge, cross the chasm
At the last, a sudden spasm
stand and limp, fall and crawl
Wick not endless in the pall
What is fair echoes hollowly
in the halls of true hallowed-be
Did the chill not warn past nest's edge?
Flight is not proof from what's in the hedge.
Stay alight, aloof, untangled
and yet hollow though unmangled.
No, the cusp, that edge, it will cleave
unwary souls within the weave
The secret now only somewhat held
is that cusp and handle are of one meld
Grasp with peril, or be its master
To gain that heaven, you must be faster.

Our Crowded Valley

Walk your road
others walk theirs
is it so hard
to see what is fair?
A stone under foot
on one not the other
of roads garners anger
but for sister or brother?
We're thrown into this
valley of roads
everyone crossing
over each other's toes
Maybe the breath
held and not free
is all that prevents
the fair sense of you and me

Refusal

Damocles' sword over everyone
In some fashion it hangs by every hair
But only some see their blood run
Don't even talk to me of fair
And if God or gods pull the puppet strings
Each line drawn back between blade and head
Should I not be indignant?
Where lies impetus other than the red?
Slavery is made of such wires
Each link in the chain a braided lock
And if we are to move from fear
What then is given up to rot?
Damn your sword and damn your trap
A pox on this pact of birthright
All these roads lead to darkness
I'll cut my path towards the light
Would that the tensile fail
If this sword should pierce my chest
The guilt shall be on thee and not me
Lest I be as guilty as all the rest

Un cer tain ty

why do you play with me?
Guessing is so impotent
What's the use of such portent?
The web that ties
us each to other
stronger, failing,
ironic mother
Are we such hummingbirds
that we can drink nothing more?
but the nectar, the milk
of our self-made whore?
The bread of civilization
now moldy crusts
our gold devalued
In that we trust?
And church bells ring
loudest in our time of fear
but there's another voice
that strains towards each ear
Not mine, but thine?
Nay, our fates intertwine.

Delusion

Glimpse through the window
the cut that bleeds
that breaks the skin
This is where we feed

Heaven and hell
are where we are
In blindness we live
within the jar

As dead, surprised?
to live is to wake
to feel every good and bad
that our hands make

Are we so in fear
of what we must feel?
Is the dream so intoxicating
that we care not what's real?

A spar marked a grave
One rope laughed wryly
The one who would walk
knew these things highly.

Belief

My cry is your cry
You just haven't voiced it
I know you feel it
waiting to surge free
Fathomless darkness
Our feeble lamps burning
Light ever touches
upon you and me
And just because some have
Bonfires burning
Should we stop seeking
Wood for other fires?
Is their light forever?
In their warmth no never?
It's all ash in the end
Our words upon pyres.

Impartialicus

Where is the Land of Unbias?
Across the Boiling Sea, they say.
The Trillion heads and twice the eyes,
The hands, like waves, clutching lies.
In this small boat I venture out
Horizons empty but for doubt.
Does a god watch over me?
Or is the mercy of the sea?
Make your way, the gales laugh
Apply your net, your hook, your gaff

Not But For Them

The screw tightens,
the vise squeezes
The rope around my neck
firmly teases
Should I be afraid anymore?
Is there really a need at the core?
Where the severed limbs of trust lay still
You'll see the remnants of my will
To play the game writ with rules
That respect not me or other fools
In the fenced-in field of slow death blowing
Its area diminished with every knowing
The rope pulls back from what is green
I'll watch the graze of others keen.

Nauta

Reaching for the nameless
We claw and grasp, drowning
Behind the veil, safe from our rendings
we wait for our return to harbor
Our vessels bear the scars
and the briny attachments
of wanderings we hardly control
Always the lighthouse burns on the high rock

Equation

The math in me
Runs a chaotic landscape
Rapid streams of intent
Gone off cliffs into seascape
Does God or other men
Abbreviate my time and space?
Which of them draws
The maps which deface?
Am I so different
From others?
Same denominator
Different numerators.
Odd, even,
Is my math a gamble?
Or maybe a test,
A divine preamble?
How ignore
The dissonant sums?
How to accept
The pain that comes?
Differing problems
Singular expectations
Where we don't meet,
Grind miscalculations.

Our Dark Monster

Judge not, unless you have numbers
Mob rules, all else encumbers
False is he who stands alone
Before the group he must atone
For being a rock within the stream
For casting a shadow before the beam
And if one has a bigger crowd
Logic is obviously the more endowed.
If I am wrong, if I'm naïve,
Then cut the fabric society weaves.

My Voice is

Cold, dark, alone
Human, sinew, bone
Confined, restrained
Breaking free, no more contained
Revenant of Truth
Less of ruth
Reflecting fire
Acidic mire
Harboring
Channeling
Accusatory
Silent oratory
Equation of
The One above
Mark the Word
It will be heard

More sunshine...

The hole below yaws bottomless
Why is not infinity above?
Nay, gravity draws back
The cosmos, speak not of.
Oblivion, no effort takes
Too ready it is to deal
Must stability bear such price
On such a gambler's wheel?
In the world of man there's
All stick and no carrot
In the world of man there's
No guarantee but for the garrote
Else you or I should see it wrong
And look to others for our bread
This contract drawn for us at birth
Is breached long and full before we're dead.

Predators

Take my coin
roll it around
There's plenty like me
to skim in this town
And it's ok
We trust the group
We're all a part of the
Social Contract troop
Altruists and cheaters
Serengeti rivals
We eat the grass and dirt
so you can have your revival
Perch on your rock
So high above Main street.
Our trust seems irrelevant
We are just so much meat.

Fog

Disbelief
Belief
Humanity on the reef
Hung on a pike
Nature's Reich
Pray for our relief?
Maker's hand
On this we stand.
In chains, rope
A violent base
A breathless race
And the hope of hope

Again

I Return
to this beach
this island
always within reach
Some I know
I've seen before
never been afraid
to knock on any door
wake your head
the sun is out
lift your voice
and let loose a shout
We're here
that's all that matters
let good and bad sort out
all we think is in tatters
Did I create this?
Or did you invoke it?
If we're going to point fingers
Let's at least make wit
What I know
is that I don't know
you don't either
so let's just let life show
us what it has
and what we need
for the next one ahead
this one's the seed.

How I feel...

Treading water
with tired limbs
Counting the hours
to reach the end
The tunnel light
keeps pace with me
always in front
Do you ken?

Recycled

We are leaves
New in spring
Dry in winter
Crumbling
Heaven, Hell
False dilemma
Both false faces
Of our schizophrenia
Somewhere
Before and behind
Where we think we see
This line of time
There's a purity
Neither happy nor sad
Tasteless water
We will and once had
Did we leave it
Unsatisfied?
Trading life
Just to die?
Am I being told
With my existence
What it is to feel
Consequence of resistance?

Blind Spot

One lost in the woods
Another has a virus
That one there is wounded
How many burned by all-of-us?
Every time we label
Good, bad, right, wrong
We mislead the lost
It's abuse by the strong
Daily we kick the wounded
Weaken the sick
Set fire to the burn ward
The smoke is thick
With the same hand
That evolution blessed
We hurl our feces
At each others' breasts
So are we better
Because some are not worse?
It's the weakest place
Where strong waters burst.

Fixed

Still small voice
As powerless as choice
What has gone before
Creates all the noise
A single decibel
But one in a symphony
My cry
A note in cacophony
Do I hear God
Inside my heart?
The culmination
of all from start?
God help me now
Or not I suppose
With predetermined
joys and woes.

Our Dream

Rise and fall
Behind, above, and fore
Can you see every little jot?
Have you evolved just to ignore?
We bang our heads
against the wall
Of our mistaken beliefs
Hoping for your call
Where do we listen?
To what goes our ear?
No graven image suits anymore
They brought us nowhere near
to the everything, the all
the hand that guides
Your answer was The Word
The shuttered lamp that hides
Do you speak in what's good?
And not in what's bad?
If so, there's very little to hear
In all the talks we've had
But maybe I'm harsh
And the fault is not thine
If I created all this,
Would the wrongs be mine?

Open

If you cannot consider the impossible,
How then the edge of what's *possible?*
What prison box contains your mind?
No more than inside can you find
That we speak from photons
Base elements become neurons
Says more on behalf of fiction
Than your limited conviction
I don't believe everything
It's enough to *receive* everything
What knocks and I do not answer
Leaves me as nothing.

Insidious

Everyone a grain of sand
Quick, wet, clinging to others
Thick mass populating
This pit of humanity bothers—
the touch of God
How can he not drowning reap?
Trying to reach the one
at bottom, deepest of deep?

Pure Water

Resonant truth
never left my side
I thought I'd left it
No, I did not abide
Weak, I stumbled
onto an ignorant path
Gave myself over
to the lesser math
Out of my stupor
of anger and fear
I'm pulled to clarity
I cannot but hear

Wish

Tell me truth is strong
That it is mighty, unassailable
That it perseveres
And all else is fallible
Paint it in purity
Sculpt its face in stone
Preach that it never loses
That it's in our very bones
Point it out boldly
Teach it to the youth
Instruct them that it conquers all
Then tell them the truth.

The Call

There's no one else
But you for someone
Standing at the edge
Like the sun
A tether
In her emptiness
The lifeline
To his happiness
All that stands
Against the end
To something
You're its only friend.
A god by any other name
Is you to someone, something
When you look up
Look down, remembering
That what you wish
For your own succor
Is another's cry
Outside the door
An animal's need
To be taken in
An insect's last chance
Before you step on him
To every thing
Its own has worth
Each mind given
Of its birth
You and I
God to the other

When we serve the lowest
We're worth the bother

Deaf

Is my voice
A thousand thunders
Crashing to earth
Already plundered?
Does the impact
move no one?
The sacrifice
all for none?
What is left
But volatility?
The last remains
Of my utility?
Every syllable
Upon the bedrock
Reverberating
In aftershock
That this world
Might reach the place
Where there's no soul
Behind the face.

This

Shine for me
Be my light
Enter day
Be gone the night
Tear the veil
Part this curtain
Let me see
What is for certain
Is nothing then?
Not even thee?
Spare me this
Dichotomy

Endless

The end is near
and the beginning too
There's a place, a point
where the crossing is two
I walk a path steady
though I ply my speed
In arrogant rebellion
I don't take heed
One can dig heel
or race on ahead
But how to avoid
that which is wed?
Can the soul flee the body
before the time's true?
The old become young?
Worn become new?
The path is the life
not the shell that contains
Water is endless
the glass just remains
Each river flowing
never the same
Step in it twice
each time a new name

Portal

What say you
from out there?
Disconnected yet
not so unfamiliar
is there a thread
between us still
a slender doorway
of light we fill
Let's tarry some
and strike the wedge
so that we might
not lose our edge

Surge

The truest question
starves for an answer
caught in the current
faster and faster
Infinity holds
it tightly bound
in the hope
that is never found
For the truest answer
need not be stated
and the very utterance
is utterly hated
Its breath, its life,
its point vierge
is to existence
a terrible surge.

The Race

Fixed, I run it anyhow
Speed will only keep me up
On my feet, not stumbling
Still, for me there is no cup.
No water to drink
No wind in my sail
Only the torrent
And fist-sized hail.
I live to live,
Hiding my gains
Lest those be also
Turned to rain.
False encouragement
A fickle lure
Stone is my face.
I must endure.
And watch the road
Paved with gold
Stretch for others,
My future sold.

Guise

This false smile
A shard in my heart
Think you can push it?
Is that your part?
Duty-bound
My path is narrow
Inevitably
This ground is fallow
Bend over the dollar
To pick up the dime
That's what it was then
And every time
Since my dollar crossed
That palm of yours
The failure hurts me
I've done nothing for.

Singularity

I am the yellow sun
burning slow, running steady
life takes its time
every moment when it's ready
I am the point verge
now, yesterday, now
tomorrow doesn't matter
take the second that is now
Tell me that this landscape
can't be mapped, can't be traveled
Tell me that we're sleeping
that we're all slowly unraveled
Are we still alive?
Do we yet run the run?
Can I hear your voice?
Am I not reaching for the sun?
The sky has no end
the earth has no center
that is not also ours
that we must not also enter
Can you say that God is not
also that which is also us?
Honesty struggles desperately
with the word in each of us.

Struggle

Why horror?
Why this threat of madness?
Endings betray short-lived good
A source for all sadness
I want to feel the sun
Forever but not every moment
Behind the veil of happiness
Lurks the ocean of torment
Is darkness our lot?
Or is our fight against it eternal?
Life, with its thin, persevering skin
Seems hopelessly maternal.

Surrender

This valley is big
and small
at the end
we see the wall
it casts a shadow
near the base
against the sun
there's no disgrace
Everyone
will stand before it
you and I
must learn to face it
but we pass through
each to the other side
and there who knows?
Go with the tide.

The Other Side

How did I get here?
Minded my own business.
Well, tried to change
Some of the nonsense.
But mostly it's not that
It's something much deeper
My uphill climb
Suddenly got steeper.
Take a side
You'll always have friends
Adhere to reason
Undoing's your end.
Yet that's almost there
But not quite
One dark moment
Is glaring in white.
In the night
Everyone's a saint
Old sun exposes
The smallest taint.
My stain is simple
Too subtle for me
Self-control must be perfect
But not equally.

Knowledge

Remember that day
When your face took in the sun?
The winds howled snow
On the ice sheet had their run
What was mortality then?
Whence the pale horse?
On the plains of those middle years
Distant trumpets had no force
Sure we watched others
Close yet almost lost
Far from our position
Their souls already touching frost
How could we not but reach
Towards what they must have felt?
And yet utterly fumble fingers
That still caused frost to melt
Did your heart feel the ghost
Of future self, free of distance?
Mine has from the first
Yet frostbite holds this instance.

Portent

It wells from within
I stare into its face
Before the surging waters
Erase this bit of grace
Mortality is meaningless
Compartmentalized existence
Try telling that
To my crippling ignorance
Loss still feels real
Every void wants to be filled
There's pain in barren earth
Where the soil was gently tilled
This wall between me and that
breached only by death
Can you say what's on the other side?
Or whether there is breath?

Devil's Bargain

Crack or die, one or the other
Sanity or life; make your barter, brother
Deep in it, peered into God's books
Tell me, should I ever have looked?
Past and future glare into the center
Through the fantasy I can never re-enter
One ... broken into infinity
Einstein, Jesus and me: quite an awkward trinity
I feel gray and colorless
Yet burned, charred, still on fire
Beauty and tragedy, both have one sire.

Duty

Teeth grit more pronounced
Jaw muscles tired
Much has changed these last few days
Let alone the weeks and months in which I've mired

Color fades to gray
Sun's rays struggle like worms through dirt
Bleak is pierced, light draws blood
It's hard to say which causes more hurt

What's unknown demands action
Who am I to decline the task?
It falls to me or no one
Regardless of how many times of God I ask

That we should be called
To usher our love through a door
So dark and silent it kills
All that will not fit its core

Seems to me absurd
Asinine, Insane
But to do aught else
appears at best profoundly profane.

Face to Face

Why does my heart beat so hard?
Because I see the cliff edge
Though it is very far
I might as well be at the ledge
Death has noticed me
Held my gaze
Time is no longer linear
I know its ways
One place we occupy
Where all places wed
If I will die, I have already
I'm filled with a sense of dread
All that I know
And what I hold dear
Eludes my forever grasp
At least that's what I fear
Maybe the veil once parted
Reveals another truth
For now I am ignorant
More so than in my youth

That's Why Babies Cry

Thrust out
Cold, wet
No more quiet contemplation
Enter into complication
Where was I before?
Somehow they've closed the door
And now I'm faced with death
From the moment of my first breath
Later is mystery
Now becomes history
I hurt because I live
And now you ask me to give
To become more
But what for?
Blessed or damned.
I am.

Reconciled

The vent is sealed
Cemented over, burned, scarred
Anger has no place here now
Dangerous emotion, explosive, hard
Again I'm different
And the standard branded on my skin
Is mine alone
Acceptable to others but for me a sin
I'm a horse
Work until done or dead
Eat my grain and be glad
Fight and take a bullet in the head
I'm a horse
All saddle and yoke
Ride, pull, or die
No complaint for the spur's bloody poke
I'm a horse
Eat my hay and be glad
Don't lay down
Don't get mad.

Intangible

My light is strong
But this place has only echoes for walls
And ghosts travel these halls
Uncertainty is what's revealed
What I've found is what I don't know
And can't see, intangible, won't show
Pain and fear make joy burn on my skin
A sensation strong that's out as much as in
If one way, why not the other?
Should not love demolish anguish, and Father rejoin Mother?

God

What?
You? Silent voice?
Surging up
Pretending choice
Treading water
Upon your wave
Could I ignore
The call I crave?
Ignorant I dwell
Straining I listen
Denied I am
The meaning seems missing
I convey
And do not hear
Is it enough
Your voice so near?

Self

A box collapsed into itself
Smaller surface-less to defend
But more surrounds—which came first?
Consequence the same; need time to mend
Outer action increased, inner slowing
Must conserve as tension's growing
Why is God so starkly silent?
Why am I a shrinking island?

Because silence forces
the teacher to emerge
You know the one
That with the familiar dirge
Listen well all your life
and yet why take the stride as if in strife?
I know me, and you know you
The sharpest wisdom is one's own knife.

FW

www.ingramcontent.com/pod-product-compliance
Lightning Source LLC
LaVergne TN
LVHW091318080426
835510LV00007B/539